THE LITTLE BOOK OF
SUPERDAD

First published in 2025 by OH
An Imprint of HEADLINE PUBLISHING GROUP LIMITED

1

Disclaimer:

Cataloguing in Publication Data is available from the British Library

ISBN 978-1-03542-256-2

Compiled and written by: Malcolm Croft
Editorial: Saneaah Muhammad
Designed and typeset in Avenir by: Andy Jones
Project manager: Russell Porter
Production: Rachel Burgess
Printed and bound in China

Headline's policy is to use papers that are natural, renewable and recyclable products and made from wood grown in well-managed forests and other controlled sources. The logging and manufacturing processes are expected to conform to the environmental regulations of the country of origin.

HEADLINE PUBLISHING GROUP LIMITED
An Hachette UK Company
Carmelite House, 50 Victoria Embankment, London EC4Y 0DZ

The authorised representative in the EEA is Hachette Ireland, 8 Castlecourt Centre, Dublin 15, D15 XTP3, Ireland (email: info@hbgi.ie)

www.headline.co.uk   www.hachette.co.uk

THE LITTLE BOOK OF

SUPER
DAD

PERFECT WORDS
FOR SUPERHERO DADS

CONTENTS

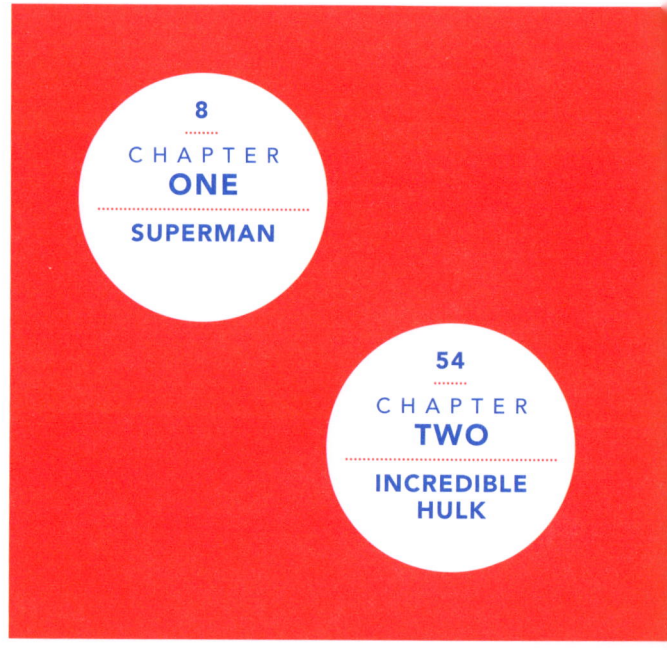

INTRODUCTION

Is it a bird? Is it a plane? No! It's just Dad dashing out the door – again! He may have forgotten where he left his keys, but give him a crisis, and he's SuperDad!

Welcome to *The Little Book of SuperDad*, a celebration of awesome dads of all shapes, sizes and ages, and a compact compendium that praises all that is great – and grating – about modern fatherhood. You see, SuperDads are not just regular dads. They're Superman, Iron Man, Batman, Thor, Mr Fantastic, Daredevil, Deadpool, Wolverine and Black Panther – with a touch of The Thing – all assembled into one snug-fitting costume. Put simply, SuperDads are the ultimate guardians of the galaxy equipped with Star-Lord's six-pack to boot.*

Inside this tiny tome, you'll find a treasure trove of trivia, quotes, lists and quips dedicated to the world's oldest unpaid and overworked profession – parenthood. It's an essential compendium for modern crime-fighting and fun-loving dads at a time when they need all the love and laughter they can get their hands on. Because, let's face it – being a dad often feels more like being unloved, unwanted and unnecessary Clark Kent than his powerful alter ego.

So, to all you SuperDads out there, this is your chance to kick off your superhero boots, hang up your cape and cover yourself in glory, one delightful page at a time. Of course, the very second you do, it'll probably be the exact moment you're called back into hero mode. But as every SuperDad knows, there's no rest for the wicked. Enjoy!

* Not a guarantee

SUPERMAN

The greatest superhero of all time, Superman is the best symbolic representation of dads ever conceived.

Think about it. Superman always turns up when you need him, and he can see, hear and smell everything. He rarely receives any gratitude (or payment) for his efforts – in fact it costs him greatly – and he wears the same unstylish clothes over and over again.

Yes, being a dad is a lot like being Superman. So, are you ready to fly?

66

Being a dad isn't just about eating a huge bag of gummy bears as your wife gives birth. It means being comfortable with the word 'hero'.

99

Ryan Reynolds
American actor

June 19, 1910

The date of the first ever Father's Day!*

It was on this day that American Sonora Smart Dodd successfully campaigned for Father's Day to be recognized as an official alternative to Mother's Day, established in 1907.

Dodd wanted to celebrate her father, civil war veteran William Jackson Smart, who raised her and her five siblings. June was chosen as it was the birthday month of Smart Senior.

So, if you want someone to blame for all your socks, ties and macaroni "artwork" – blame Sonora Smart Dodd!

* In the US, Canada and the UK, Father's Day is celebrated on the third Sunday in June. In Australia and New Zealand, it's celebrated on the first Sunday of September.

85 per cent

The percentage of U.S. fathers who consider being a dad the best job in the world – and the most important aspect of their life.

The remaining 15 per cent are clearly not SuperDads!

*"By Saint Mary, my lady,
Your mammy and daddy
Brought forth a goodly baby!"*
(It goes on... a lot.)

According to the Oxford English Dictionary, the word "daddy" was first recorded in 1523, in a poem called "To Mistress Isabell Pennell" by the English poet John Skelton – a tutor to King Henry VIII, no less.

Today, scholars agree that the origin of the word "dada" descends from nonsensical baby gibberish.

What did the drummer name his twin daughters?

Anna One! Anna Two!

> **"**
> You don't have to
> be perfect to be a
> perfect parent.
> **"**

Michael Sullivan, *Road to Perdition* **(2002)**
Directed by Sam Mendes

Shakespeare's the Daddy

William Shakespeare, the world's greatest playwright and a father of three, had a lot to say about parenting... *most* of it positive.

"Who would be a father!"

Othello, Act 1, Scene 1

"Why, 'tis a happy thing
To be the father unto many sons."

Henry VI: Part 3, Act 3, Scene 2

"My father's wit, and my mother's
tongue, assist me!"

Love's Labour's Lost, Act 1, Scene 2

"O, that our fathers would applause our loves,
To seal our happiness with their consents!"
Two Gentlemen of Verona, Act 1, Scene 3

"To you your father should be as a god,
One that composed your beauties, yea, and one
To whom you are but as a form in wax,
By him imprinted and within his power,
To leave the figure or disfigure it."
A Midsummer Night's Dream, Act 1, Scene 1

"If by chance I talk a little wild, forgive me;
I had it from my father."
Henry VIII, Act 1, Scene 4

"It is a wise father that knows his own child."
Merchant Of Venice, Act 2, Scene 2

You Know You're a SuperDad When...

You find yourself unable to answer a child's question and simply tell them, "Go ask your mother."

SuperDad Cocktail #1: Long Island Iced Tea

The best cocktail for SuperDads on Father's Day – the Long Island Iced Tea! This super-boozy cocktail will ensure all SuperDads end the day as they deserve: slumped on the sofa, fast asleep!

45 ml (1.5 oz) vodka
45 ml (1.5 oz) gin
45 ml (1.5 oz) tequila
45 ml (1.5 oz) rum
45 ml (1.5 oz) triple sec

45 ml (1.5 oz) fresh lime juice
Ice
Cola (fill to the top)
2 limes, cut into wedges

Pour the spirits into a large jug and add the lime juice. Add half a jug of ice and stir, before adding the cola and stirring some more. Throw in the ` lime wedges and divide into highball glasses. Stir. Sip. Snooze.

Be More Vader

Darth Vader is the best SuperDad in the galaxy. Think about it. Like all fathers, he became evil at precisely the same time as his children were born. He even called himself Darth Vader, German for "Dark Father", just to make his parenting limitations clear from the offset.

Vader then spent the next 30 years keeping his twin children safe from a megalomaniacal emperor – only for his idiot son, Luke, to travel half-way across the galaxy hellbent on destroying him. After reverting to the light side of the Force, Vader died while trying to save his son's life – who burnt his body on an open flame to say thanks!

Then, while all of this father-son bonding was going on, Vader's daughter, Leia, never once called to say hello – despite receiving gifts of some truly awesome superpowers. Kids, huh!

66

No...
I am your father.

99

Darth Vader, *The Empire Strikes Back* (1980)
Directed by Irvin Kershner

SuperDad Playlist #1
Essentials

1. *Daughters*, John Mayer
2. *Beautiful Boy*, John Lennon
3. *Song for Dad*, Keith Urban
4. *Dance With My Father*, Luther Vandross
5. *My Daddy Knows Best*, The Marvelettes
6. *Song For My Father*, Sarah McLachlan
7. *Daddy Lessons*, Beyoncé & Dixie Chicks
8. *Let Me Be The Man My Daddy Was*, The Chi-Lites
9. *The Greatest Man I Never Knew*, Reba McEntire
10. *Living Years*, Mike and the Mechanics

SuperDad Advice #1

To keep your sanity, you need to develop "Dad vision" – the ability to step over rogue Lego blocks, ignore spattered walls and pretend the dishes aren't piling up.

Embrace it – it's your superpower.

What do you call a cow on a trampoline?

A milk shake!

Dad's the Word

While the word "father" originates from the ye Olde English word *fæder* (meaning "supreme being", naturally), the word "dad" comes from "dada", the sound made by infants attempting to speak soft consonants.

"Dada" is the most natural sound an infant can make (it requires no mouth muscle movement), and is often uttered before "mama".

66

When you're young,
you think your dad is
Superman. Then you
grow up, and you realize
he's just a regular guy
who wears a cape.

99

Dave Attell
American comedian

You Know You're a Parent When...

You realize the cruel
irony of the phrase
"sleeps like a baby".

66

When your wife is pregnant and you're expecting, everyone is like, 'It's incredible. Get ready, it's magic. It's the most life-changing experience you'll ever have. Brace yourself for heaven.' And then the second the baby comes, everyone is like, 'WELCOME TO HELL.'

99

Andy Samberg
American actor

SuperDad Motto #1

Raising a strong child
requires a strong drink.

Top Ten SuperDads

Instead of watching our kids, we watched a load of movies and TV, and we've decided these are the greatest SuperDads on the big and small screens. Do you agree?

Movies

Marlin, *Finding Nemo*

Jonathan Kent, *Man of Steel*

George Bailey,
It's a Wonderful Life

Papa Elf, *Elf*

Richard Williams,
King Richard

Gomez Addams,
The Addams Family

Thomas Wayne, *Batman*

Bryan Mills, *Taken*

Daniel Hillard,
Mrs Doubtfire

Vito Corleone,
The Godfather

TV

Hal Wilkerson,
Malcolm in the Middle

Jim Hopper, *Stranger Things*

Mike Brady, *The Brady Bunch*

Rick Grimes,
The Walking Dead

Phil Dunphy, *Modern Family*

Michael Bluth,
Arrested Development

Tony Soprano, *The Sopranos*

Bob Belcher, *Bob's Burgers*

Ron Swanson,
Parks and Recreation

Homer Simpson,
The Simpsons

"

Never raise your hand to your kids. It leaves your groin unprotected.

"

Red Buttons
American comedian

SuperDads are the Best.*

* They always say "Yes" when Mum says "No."

SuperDad Motto #2

Do not negotiate
with terrorists.

SuperDad Movie Playlist
Classics

Father's Day (1997)

Mr Mom (1983)

Parenthood (1989)

National Lampoon's Vacation (1983)

Father of the Bride (1991)

Indiana Jones and the Last Crusade (1989)

The Parent Trap (1998)

Mrs Doubtfire (1993)

Cheaper by the Dozen (2003)

Three Men and a Baby (1987)

> ## You are the best thing I ever created... I love you 3,000.

Tony Stark, *Avengers: Endgame* (2019)
Directed by Anthony and Joe Russo

❝

Dads are most
ordinary men turned
by love into heroes,
adventurers, storytellers
and singers of song.

❞

Pam Brown
Australian poet

SuperDad Cocktail #2:
The Deep Sleep

It's 7 pm. The baby's down for the night.
You've got 12 hours to party. Celebrate with a
cocktail known as The Deep Sleep. It'll have
you in bed, lights out, by 7.30 pm.

- Three shots of whisky
- Two tablespoons of hot chocolate powder
- A mug of warm milk.

Mix the three shots of your favourite whisky
into a mug filled with warm milk. Add the two
tablespoons of hot chocolate powder. Stir.
Add a big dollop of squirty cream to really
slow the senses. Good night.

SuperDad Motto #3

Silence is golden.
Unless you have kids.
Then it's suspicious.

"

Drive carefully. And don't forget to fasten your condom.

"

George Banks, *Father of the Bride* (1991)
Directed by Charles Shyer

Be More Homer

Never has a father loved his children so unconditionally, and yet been so indifferent to raising them properly, as the world's greatest SuperDad, Homer Simpson.

Here's why...

"Kids, you tried your best and you failed miserably. The lesson is, never try."

"Burns Heir"

Season 5, Episode 18, 1994

"Marriage is like a coffin and each kid is another nail."

"Eight Misbehavin"

Season 14, Episode 2, 1999

"The key to parenting is don't overthink it. Because overthinking leads to... what were we talking about?"

"The Burns Cage"

Season 27, Episode 17, 2016

"Son, if you really want something in this life, you have to work for it. Now quiet! They're about to announce the lottery numbers."
"Bart Gets an Elephant"
Season 5, Episode 17, 1994

"Marge, don't discourage the boy! Weaselling out of things is important to learn. It's what separates us from the animals! Except the weasel."
"Boy-Scoutz 'n the Hood"
Season 5, Episode 8, 1994

"It's not easy to juggle a pregnant wife and a troubled child, but somehow I managed to fit in eight hours of TV a day."
"Lisa's First Word"
Season 4, Episode 10, 1992

"Kids are the best. You can teach them to hate the things you hate. And they practically raise themselves, what with the Internet and all."
"Bart Star"
Season 9, Episode 6, 1994

SuperDad Advice #2

Master the "Dad Nap"
technique.

Don't wait for everyone to
leave you alone to catch
40 winks – just close your eyes,
remote in hand, and call it
"resting your eyes".

"

Hello. My name is Inigo Montoya. You killed my father. Prepare to die.

"

Inigo Montoya, *The Princess Bride* (1987)
Directed by Rob Reiner

$23 billion

In 2024, the amount spent in total by the

75 per cent

of Americans who celebrate Father's Day, according to *The Shelf*, 2024.

For context, NASA's annual budget is exactly the same.

"

I've done all kinds of cool things as an actor: I've jumped out of helicopters and done some daring stunts and played baseball in a professional stadium, but none of it means anything compared to being somebody's daddy.

"

Chris Pratt
American actor

Couvade Syndrome

Good news for expecting SuperDads – you're not getting fat. (Well, you are. But it's not your fault.*) You're just another victim of *Couvade Syndrome*, or sympathetic pregnancy pains – an emotional response to preparing for parenthood.

The symptoms include: indigestion, weight gain, fatigue, food cravings, vomiting, diarrhoea, constipation, nausea, mood swings, stomach pain, bloating, cramping, headache, backache, toothache.

(So, basically, one big hangover.)

* Possibly. Some believe Couvade Syndrome is psychosomatic.

> **"**
>
> There's no manual
> for being a great dad.
> Believe me, if there was,
> I would've lost it already.
>
> **"**

Michael Kyle, *My Wife and Kids* **(2005)**

66

If you're not yelling at your kids, you aren't spending enough time with them.

99

Mark Ruffalo
American actor

You Know You're a SuperDad When...

You're scared to sit down and get comfortable because you know it'll only be a matter of seconds before all hell breaks loose.

A 2014 University of British Columbia study revealed that SuperDads who do household chores tend to have more professionally ambitious daughters, as well as daughters with broader definitions of gender roles.

Get cleaning, guys!

"

Father to a murdered son, husband to a murdered wife, and I will have my vengeance, in this life or the next.

"

Maximus Decimus Meridius, *Gladiator* **(2000)**
Directed by Ridley Scott

Immortal Words:
SuperDad Edition #1

1. "Don't make me come in there!"

2. "Go ask your Mum."

3. "No means no."

4. "I'm not going to repeat myself again."

5. "Shhh! Don't tell Mum."

6. "I'm cleverer than I look, you know."

7. "Because I said so, that's why."

8. "When I was a boy, I didn't have half as much as you do now."

9. "You don't know the meaning of the word 'bored'."

10. "When I was a boy…"

You Know You're a SuperDad When...

You consider a sleeping baby a higher high than any Happy Hour or wild night out you've ever had.

INCREDIBLE HULK

There's no denying it - SuperDads look, behave and smell a lot like the Incredible Hulk, the strongest of all superheroes.

They're big, lumpy and clumsy, too, and they're prone to rage (especially when driving) and turning green (when they can't go to the pub).

Yeah, SuperDads are Hulks. So, without further ado, it's smashing time!

You Know You're a SuperDad When...

You start wearing slippers.

Not because you feel elderly, but because of all the sharp objects on the floor that could stab you.

22 million

The number of Father's Day cards sent in the UK in 2022, approximately one-third of the entire British population.

In the U.S.,

72 million

Father's Day cards were sent, roughly one-fifth of the population.

Source: Hallmark Corporate, 2022

"

Twelve weeks old: when your kid is young enough to fall asleep on your chest yet long enough to kick you in the nuts at the same time.

"

Lin-Manuel Miranda
American director and musician

You Know You're a SuperDad When...

You book a weekend break to have time away from your kids... and then miss them every day.

11 per cent

The percentage of dads who, for a Father's Day gift, just wanted to be left alone and have a day to themselves.*

According to Statista, 2024

SuperDad Motto #4

Measure twice, cut once, but probably still buy extra. (For all you DIY Dads).

71 per cent

The percentage of 21st-century fathers who use social media such as YouTube, X and TikTok to get advice and information on how to be better dads – according to Statista, 2024.

Children with SuperDads are 80 per cent less likely to spend time in prison, 75 per cent less likely to have a teen birth and 43 per cent more likely to do better at school.*

Don't stop being a SuperDad!

According to the University of Cambridge, 2023

What kind of noise does a witch's vehicle make?

Brrrrooooom, broooooom

"

Actually, I was a wonderful father. Did I ever tell you to eat up? Go to bed? Wash your ears? Do your homework? No. I respected your privacy, and I taught you self-reliance.

"

Henry Jones, *Indiana Jones and the Last Crusade* **(1991)**
Directed by Steven Spielberg

Back to the Future

This 1985 sci-fi blockbuster is the perfect Father's Day movie for SuperDads. The film sees Marty McFly (Michael J. Fox) travel back in time to 1955, where he becomes the object of his teen mother's not-so-maternal affections – and must find a way to bring his future parents back together.

"Wait a minute. Are you trying to tell me that my mother has got the hots for me?"

Marty McFly, *Back to the Future* **(1985)**
Directed by Robert Zemeckis

Daedalus, the creator of the labyrinth (you know, the huge maze located under the court of King Minos of Crete, where the monstrous Minotaur lived) is not the most famous father in Greek mythology. But he is, perhaps, one of the most caring.

Daedalus told his first-born son, Icarus, to wax his wings before his infamous flight (too close) to the sun. Naturally, Icarus didn't listen – and paid the price.

The moral of this story?
Daddies know best.

In February 2020, the world said goodbye to 104-year-old father-of-two Ramjit Raghav. This SuperDad was

aged 96

when he became a parent to his second son, Ranjeet* .

His first son was born when Ramjit was... 94!

43 per cent

The percentage of SuperDads who agreed that their favourite parenting years were when their children were aged between six and 12.

Only 13 per cent thought the teenage years, 13–17, were best.*

According to a 2015 Active Families, Happy Families survey

"

I will be watching you and if
I find that you are trying to
corrupt my first-born child, I will
bring you down, baby. I will bring
you down to Chinatown.

"

Jack Byrnes, *Meet The Parents* **(2000)**
Directed by Jay Roach

18 per cent

The percentage increase of UK dads carrying out unpaid childcare in the aftermath of the COVID-19 pandemic – according to the Fatherhood Institute (2022).

Damn you, coronavirus!

They say parents would move mountains for their children. Dendi Sherpa did the next best thing – he climbed one with his 16-year-old daughter, Ngim Chhamji Sherpa. The first (and only) father-daughter combo to reach the peak of Mount Everest at the same time, the Nepalese duo achieved the feat on May 19, 2012.

* Sir Edmund Hillary created history on May 29, 1953 when he became the first person to ascend the summit of Mount Everest. His son, Peter, also reached the peak – in 1990.

Doodad / *du–dad*

noun

A gadget or object whose name the speaker does not know or cannot recall.

"Has anyone seen the, er, doodad that turns the TV on?"*

* Named after forgetful dads, no doubt

According to
Pew Research 2023,
only six U.S. men
identified themselves as
stay-at-home parents in the 1970s.
Not six per cent – six men!

Today, one in five stay-at-home
parents in the U.S. are dads –
more than
2.4 million men.
Super stay-at-home Dads,
we salute you!

You Know You're a SuperDad When...

You find yourself watching entire movies while sitting on the toilet.

Anything for a moment of peace and quiet.

Immortal Words:
SuperDad Edition #2

1. "Fight amongst yourselves."

2. "You're going out looking like that?"

3. "In my day, we used our imaginations."

4. "There's nothing a little brute force can't fix."

5. "My house, my rules..."

6. "I paid good money for that!"

7. "Don't spend it all at once."

8. "They don't make them like they used to."

9. "What's the damage?"

10. "That's how they get you."

Across the world,
SuperDads are called a variety
of names.

1. Filipino –
Taytay

2. Arabic – *Baba*

3. Spanish – *Papá*

4. Swahili – *Baba*

5. Slovak – *Otec*

6. Polish – *Tata*

7. Portuguese –
Pai

8. Nepali – *Buwa*

9. Maori –
Haakoro

10. Mandarin
Chinese – *Baba*

11. Korean – *Appa*

12. Japanese –
Otōsan

13. Italian – *Babbo*

14. Hindi – *Pita-ji*

15. French – *Papa*

"

When I was six years old, my father said to me... 'Get out!'

"

Lex Luthor, *Superman* (1978)
Directed by Richard Donner

SuperDad Playlist #2
Classics

1. *My Father's Eyes*, Eric Clapton
2. *Wind Beneath My Wings*, Eddie Levert
3. *Teach Your Children*, Crosby, Stills, Nash & Young
4. *Papa Don't Preach*, Madonna
5. *Papa's Got A Brand New Bag*, James Brown
6. *My Father's House*, Bruce Springsteen
7. *Cat's In The Cradle*, Harry Chapin
8. *Father And Son*, Yusuf Islam / Cat Stevens
9. *Daddy's Working Boots*, Dolly Parton
10. *He Walked On Water*, Randy Travis

"

The worst part about being a parent is when one of your kids farts and you have to pretend it wasn't cool.

"

Rob Delaney
American comedian

What did the horse say after it tripped?

Help! I've fallen and I can't giddyup!

"

You know what it's like
having a fourth kid?
Imagine you're drowning,
then someone hands
you a baby.

"

Jim Gaffigan
American comedian

"

A man who doesn't spend time with his family can never be a real man.

"

Vito Corleone, *The Godfather* (1972)
Directed by Francis Ford Coppola

$312,202

The cost of raising
one child from birth to age 18,
according to the U.S. Bureau of
Labor Statistics.

In the UK, the figure is

£223,256

according to *Metro*, 2024.

SuperDad #2

In 1949, Candido Jacuzzi's 15-month-old son developed rheumatoid arthritis. It was discovered that hydrotherapy considerably relieved his pain – but unfortunately, the nearest hospital with a suitable unit was many miles away.

Candido set about devising a whirlpool bath in the family bathtub. A year later, he had patented his invention and sold it for medical use. You'll never guess what he called it?*

A jacuzzi... if you didn't get that

Be More Bandit

Bluey and Bingo's doggy dad, Bandit – from the hit TV cartoon *Bluey* – shows us all how to be a proper SuperDad. Here are Bandit's best bits:

"I am not Dad. I am Magic Claw. Magic Claw has no children, his days are free and easy."
"Magic Claw", Season 1, Episode 22, 2019

"You're braver than you believe, stronger than you seem and smarter than you think."
"Flat Pack", Season 2, Episode 21, 2020

"This is all my stuff, from when I used to be cool."
"The Dump", Season 1, Episode 44, 2019

"I just need 30 minutes on the couch!"
"Yoga Ball", Season 2, Episode 7, 2020

"I'm kind of a dodgy Dad."
"Grannies", Season 1, Episode 28, 2019

SuperDad Playlist #3
Special Bond

1. *I'm Her Daddy*, Bill Withers
2. *I Learned From You*, Billy Ray & Miley Cyrus
3. *Sweet Child O' Mine*, Guns 'n' Roses
4. *Daddy Could Swear, I Declare*, Gladys Knight and the Pips
5. *They Don't Make 'Em Like My Daddy Anymore*, Loretta Lynn
6. *Colour Him Father*, The Winstons
7. *Father And Daughter*, Paul Simon
8. *Father To Son*, Queen
9. *Papa Was A Rolling Stone*, The Temptations
10. *Letter 2 My Unborn*, Tupac Shakur

Fatherhood:

Banging your head
against a
very cute and loveable
brick wall.

"

Do or do not.
There is no try.

"

Yoda, *Star Wars: The Empire Strikes Back* (1980)
Directed by Irvin Kershner

What kind of dinosaur loves to sleep?

A stega-snore-us

66

I'm a cool dad, that's my thang.
I'm hip, I surf the web, I text. LOL:
laugh out loud, OMG: Oh my god,
WTF: Why the face...

99

Phil Dunphy, *Modern Family*,
"Game Changer", Season 1, Episode 19 (2010)

66

I cannot think of any need in childhood as strong as the need for a father's protection.

99

Sigmund Freud
Austrian neurologist and the founder
of psychoanalysis

SuperDad #3

The thirty-third president of the USA,
Harry Truman, was a proud father.
In 1950, after a *Washington Post* music
critic gave his daughter, Margaret, a
negative review for a singing performance,
Truman responded in a less than
presidential manner:
"Someday I hope to meet you. When that
happens, you'll need a new nose and a lot
of beefsteak for black eyes…"

"

When I was a young man, I thought life was all about me. But then my daughters came into my world with all their curiosity and mischief and those smiles that never fail to fill my heart and light up my day. And suddenly, all my big plans for myself didn't seem so important anymore. I soon found that the greatest joy in my life was the joy I saw in theirs.

"

Barack Obama
Forty-fourth president of the United States

SuperDad TV Playlist
Staples

The Sopranos (1999–2007)

Top Gear (2002–22)

Band of Brothers (2001)

Only Fools and Horses (1981–2003)

The Wire (2002–08)

Seinfeld (1989–98)

Sherlock (2010–17)

Breaking Bad (2008–13)

The West Wing (1999–2006)

Peaky Blinders (2013–2022)

Modern SuperDads spend seven times more time playing and interacting with their children than their own fathers did with them 40 years ago, according to a 2014 report from the University of London and the University of Seville.

The research also highlighted that dads in the mid-1970s spent as little as five minutes a day playing with their children.

66

I feel like I'm running
a small nursery with
someone I used to date.

99

Jesse Wallace, *Before Sunset* (2004)
Directed by Richard Linklater

78 per cent

The percentage of women who think the Dad Bod* is "sexy" and a sign that a man is confident in his own skin, according to a PlanetFitness study in 2024.

* Dad Bods, reflecting the perfect balance between irregular exercise and outright laziness, belong to SuperDads who "can" be active but eat and drink whatever the hell they want.

Top Ten Superbad Dads

Some dads are anything but super. What about this lot for starters?

1. Logan Roy, *Succession*

2. Mr Wormwood, *Matilda*

3. Daniel Plainview, *There Will Be Blood*

4. Al Bundy, *Married With Children*

5. Frank Gallagher, *Shameless*

6. George Bluth Sr, *Arrested Development*

7. Jack Torrance, *The Shining*

8. Frank Reynolds, *It's Always Sunny in Philadelphia*

9. Tywin Lannister, *Game of Thrones*

10. Walter White, *Breaking Bad*

MR
FANTASTIC

Hailing from one of the most important comic books of all time, Mr Fantastic is the super heroic alter-ego of Richard Reed, the leader of The Fantastic Four.

Reed is, of course, a stereotypical father gifted with a hyper-elastic body and a super-hot wife – and he considers himself the smartest man in the entire universe.

Sound familiar?

24 per cent

According to
PewResearch.org, 2024,
the percentage of children
financially* independent
by the age of 22.

*Sorry to be the one to break it to you but SuperDads will
be stuck looking after their kids' finances until they're
SuperDead.*

Fatherhood:

Like marriage.
But without the tax
breaks.

Why do hills never become mountains?

Because they peak too soon

Fatherhood:

Just when you
get the hang of it –
everything
changes.

> 66

I hope I can be as good a dad to you as my dad was to me.

> 99

Mufasa, *The Lion King* (1994)
Directed by Rob Minkoff and Roger Allers

> **"**
>
> By the time a man
> realizes that maybe
> his father was right, he
> usually has a son who
> thinks he's wrong.
>
> **"**

Charles Wadsworth
American musician

Did you hear about the claustrophobic astronaut?

He needed a little more space

"

When your children are teenagers, it's important to have a dog so that someone in the house is happy to see you.

"

Nora Ephron
American screenwriter

Smile
because you love them.

Laugh
because you're too tired
to cry.

Drink
because you can.

66

To be the father of growing daughters is to understand that your heart is running around inside someone else's body. It also makes me quite astonishingly calm at the thought of death: I know whom I would die to protect.

99

Christopher Hitchens
British author

> **"**
>
> It was times like these when I thought my father, who hated guns and had never been to any wars, was the bravest man who ever lived.
>
> **"**

Harper Lee
To Kill a Mockingbird, 1960

"

Father! To God
Himself we cannot give
a holier name.

"

William Wordsworth
Ecclesiastical Sonnets, 1821–22

What's the leading cause of dry skin?

Towels

SuperDad Motto #5

Bedtime is a marathon,
not a sprint.

> **"**
>
> # Nemo, I look at you, and I'm home.
>
> **"**

Marlin, *Finding Nemo* (2003)
Directed by Andrew Stanton and Lee Unkrich

"

My father had a
profound influence on
me. He was a lunatic.

"

Spike Milligan
British comedian

You Know You're a SuperDad When....

You wake up one morning in your forties, look in the mirror at your face, body and clothes, and realize you've become your dad.

Don't Panic!*

Other SuperDads don't know what they're doing either.

69

The number of children
Russian peasant Feodor Vasilyev
(1707-82) fathered to just

one (poor, poor) woman.

Among this throng were four
sets of quadruplets, seven sets of
triplets and 16 pairs of twins.

You Know You're a SuperDad When...

You catch yourself asking your children, "You call that music?" when they play the latest tunes.

It's a phrase you can hear your own dad saying...

Evolutionary biologist Charles Darwin was a huge fan of passing on his DNA – and not necessarily always for scientific purposes.

He was a doting dad to 10 children.

What do you call a hen looking at a lettuce?

Chicken Ceaser Salad

According to an article published by CBS News, 2011, the earliest inscribed record of a Father's Day "card" dates back 4,000 years.

The clay tablet, found in the ruins of Babylon (modern-day Iraq), was carved with a stylus by a young boy called Elmesu.

In the message, he wishes his father good health and a long life.

You Know You're a SuperDad When...

You remind your children of your superpowers with the classic threat, "Just remember – I've got eyes in the back of my head."

"

Know thy enemy and know yourself; in a hundred battles, you will never be defeated. When you are ignorant of the enemy but know yourself, your chances of winning or losing are equal. If ignorant both of your enemy and of yourself, you are sure to be defeated in every battle.

"

Sun Tzu
Chinese general and military strategist

A study by the University of North Carolina found that humans are more genetically similar to their fathers than they are to their mothers.

Even though we inherit the same number of genetic mutations from both parents, we use 10 per cent more of our fathers' DNA.

Source: *Time* Magazine, 2015

SuperDad Advice #3

Remember, a toolbox is often just for show.

When in doubt about a faulty appliance, just tap something, mutter, "It's probably the flux capacitor", and go online to find a solution later.

What do you call two guys hanging out by your window?

Kurt & Rod

> **"**
>
> Kids are creepy. What happens if I wake up in the middle of the night, look over and my child is standing in the doorway? Do I run? Which direction do I run? Towards it? Away from it?
>
> **"**

Jordan Peele
American director

"

Fathering is not something perfect men do, but something that perfects the man. The end product of child-raising is not the child but the parent.

"

Frank Pittman
American author

Fatherhood is like baking a cake.

A really ungrateful, whiny and expensive cake.

A SuperDad
consumes, on average,
300 more calories a day
than a non-parent.*

It's usually leftovers and
mainly stress-eating.

*Thankfully, a SuperDad also burns more than 500 calories
a day than a non-parent – often from pursuing an
escaped toddler.*

"

I think every kid thinks their dad is goofy. Even Johnny Depp's kid must be like, 'Oh my God, my dad with those freakin' scarves. This isn't a pirate ship; it's a Costco, Dad.'

"

Judd Apatow
American director

What do you get when you put a sheep on a trampoline?

A woolly jumper

You Know You're a SuperDad When...

You see something broken in your home and think to yourself, "I'll fix that later."

"

Anyone who tells
you fatherhood is the
greatest thing that can
happen to you, they are
understating it.

"

Mike Myers
American actor

Immortal Words:
SuperDad Edition #3

1. "Ready to rock and roll?"

2. "One day, you'll thank me."

3. "I brought you into this world, and I can take you out of it."

4. "A little hard work never hurt anybody."

5. "No one said life was fair."

6. "Ask a stupid question, you'll get a stupid answer."

7. "Act your age, not your shoe size."

8. "I'll do it this once and this once only."

9. "Is there anything else you'd like me to do? Peel you a grape?"

10. "It's like talking to a brick wall!"

SuperDad #5

Author J.R.R. Tolkien was a dedicated dad to his three sons and a daughter. In order not to miss out on quality time with them, he wrote his fantasy stories before sunrise each day.

Several stories from his masterpieces – *The Hobbit* and *The Lord of the Rings* – began as improvised bedtime stories told to his children.

66

The heart of a father is the masterpiece of nature.

99

Abbé Prévost
*The Story of the Chevalier des Grieux
and Manon Lescaut,* 1731

A study by the National Institute of Health discovered that expectant fathers exhibited prenatal decreases in testosterone and oestradiol (a form of oestrogen) just by thinking about fatherhood.

Furthermore, the study showed that men with larger declines in testosterone were more engaged with the raising of their babies.

Overall, dads experience a 34 per cent decrease in testosterone during the first five years of their child's life.

Source: National Library of Medicine, 2017

What did the
alien say to
the gardener?

Take me to your weeder

"

I would say that the hardest thing about being a parent is these goddamned kids.

Andy Richter
American actor and comedian

> **"**
>
> Any fool with a dick can make a baby, but only a real man can raise his children.
>
> **"**

Jason Furious Styles, *Boyz n the Hood* **(1991)**
Directed by John Singleton

The Father Effect

The "Father Effect" is a known phenomenon where children are more likely to excel when their dad is present in their lives. It remains roughly equal for boys and girls from birth until puberty.

Studies have shown that teenage daughters* take much fewer sexual risks if they have strong relationships with their dads.

Sons... not so much.

Source: Dads4Life.com, 2022

THE JOKER

For centuries – perhaps even millennia –
SuperDads have been showing off their
top-tier sense of humour by telling their
children "dad jokes".

No point in denying it – SuperDads are the
funniest member of the family.

With a seemingly never-ending arsenal of
wit and wisdom at their disposal, it's time
to say hello to… The Joker.

If you're ever feeling exhausted, frustrated and poor – don't panic!

According to a 2023 CBS News report,

90 per cent

of the time you spend with your kids in your lifetime will be finished

by the time they're 18.

From the day your children leave home, you'll spend just one more year with them in total.

> 66
>
> There's no such thing as ready. You just jump on a moving train and you try not to die.
>
> 99

Jules Baxter, *What To Expect When You're Expecting* **(2012)**
Directed by Kirk Jones

In the middle ages, women believed they had more chance of siring a son if they asked their husbands to turn their faces eastwards* during sex.

*Most medieval men would, presumably, have been fine with this arrangement – it's less awkward than eye contact, after all.

You Know You're a SuperDad When...

All your passwords are your children's birthdays – which everyone you know, knows.*

To be fair, these are the only dates you can definitely remember. (Until the kids turn 20 at least.)

You Know You're a SuperDad When...

You mutter
the immortal words:
"I'm not lost,
I'm just taking the
scenic route."

The 1967 hit single "Something Stupid" by Frank Sinatra and his daughter Nancy remains the only father-daughter collaboration in music history to reach the No.1 spot.

> **"**
>
> Don't worry that children never listen to you; worry that they are always watching you.
>
> **"**

Robert Fulghum
American author

Vatertag

Welcome to Germany's very own twist on Father's Day – *Vatertag*, or *Männertag* (Gentlemen's Day).

Celebrated every May, *Vatertag* is a well-deserved day-off for SuperDads that goes way beyond a standard Father's Day.

Instead of spending the day with their families, groups of men parade through the countryside pulling handcarts loaded with beer and snacks.

4.4 lbs

The number of pounds a new dad puts on in weight, on average, in his child's first year – a 2.6 per cent rise in BMI, according to a study reported in the *Daily Mail*, 2015.

"

Everybody in the car.
Boat leaves in two minutes. Or,
perhaps you don't want to see
the second-largest ball of twine
on the face of the earth, which is
only four short hours away.

"

Clark Griswold, *National Lampoon's Vacation* (1983)
Directed by Harold Ramis

100 million

The number of sperm a man releases each time he ejaculates. Only a few hundred of these will reach a female's egg – and the egg has special receptors to ensure only one sperm is allowed in.

So, next time your son or daughter scratches the car, drops soup on the floor or elbows you in the eye-socket – just remember, they are a one-in-100-million miracle!

You Know You're a SuperDad When...

You'd rather eat in than out.

The thought of two hours round a table with screaming, food-throwing kids – while strangers look on – is just too much to bear!

86

The number of Lego bricks for every man, woman and child on Earth, according to the Museum of Science and Industry, 2024.

It's estimated that a SuperDad will tread on approximately 52 pieces of Lego during his parenting life*, causing him to scream blue murder each and every time. But there's a reason for this!

A single, two-by-two Lego brick can withstand up to 950 pounds of pressure. Because the Lego doesn't collapse when you step on it, the pressure of your weight is forced back up into your foot, causing immense pain. And, with more than 200,000 sensory receptors in each sole, your poor feet are incredibly sensitive to pain!

OK, we made this up. But the actual number is probably a lot higher!

Next time you feel lost
and alone – and reeling
from being elbowed in
the groin – remember
there are 1.5 billion other
fathers currently living in
the world who have felt
your pain.

Immortal Words:
SuperDad Edition #4

1. "You make a better door than a window."

2. "Where was it the last place you left it?"

3. "You can't make a silk purse out of a sow's ear."

4. "Money doesn't grow on trees."

5. "Don't use that tone with me."

6. "Do you think I'm made of money?"

7. "What did your last slave die of?"

8. "I'm not your chauffeur."

9. "I'm not sleeping, I'm just resting my eyes."

10. "I heard that."

66

If you bungle raising
your children, I don't
think whatever else you
do matters very much.

99

Jacqueline Kennedy
Former First Lady of the United States

You Know You're a SuperDad When...

You give your children wildly flamboyant-yet-practical advice, such as, "If your friend jumped off a bridge, would you do it too?"

> **❝**
>
> Sometimes I am amazed that my wife and I created two human beings from scratch yet struggle to assemble the most basic of IKEA cabinets.
>
> **❞**

Greg Kinnear
American actor

66

Listen, you're my children and I love you, but you're all terrible at what you do here and I feel like I should tell you. I'd fire all of you if I could.

99

Bob Belcher, *Bob's Burgers,* **"Human Flesh",
Season 1, Episode 1 (2011)**
Written by Loren Bouchard

SuperDad Advice #4

Remember to take a shower every day.

Your kids can smell your fear.

Why was
the broom late
for work?

It overswept

> You will carry me inside you, all the days of your life. You will make my strength your own, and see my life through your eyes, as your life will be seen through mine. The son becomes the father, and the father the son. This is all I can send you, Kal-El.

Jor-El, *Superman* (1979)
Directed by Richard Donner

> **"**
>
> Just remember these
> two things: she's
> 19 years old, and the 82nd
> Airborne works for me.
>
> **"**

President Bartlet, *The West Wing,*
"Lord John Marbury", Season 1, Episode 11 (2000)

What do you
get when
two giraffes
collide?

A giraffic jam

> **"**
>
> My dad used to say, 'Always fight fire with fire.' Which is probably why he got thrown out of the fire brigade.
>
> **"**

Harry Hill
British comedian

> **Just taught my kids about taxes by eating 38 per cent of their ice cream.**

Conan O'Brien
American comedian

66

I'm just trying to be a father, raise a daughter and a son, be a lover to their mother, everything to everyone.

99

Chris Gardner, *The Pursuit of Happyness* (2006)
Directed by Gabriele Muccino

SuperDad Motto #6

Be the last one to laugh –
just in case nobody else
appreciates your
dad jokes.

> **"**
>
> Having children is like living in a frat house – nobody sleeps, everything's broken and there's a lot of throwing up.
>
> **"**

Ray Romano
American comedian

SuperDad Advice #5

Buy yourself some noise-cancelling headphones – these babies will be your secret weapon.

Toddler tantrums? Kids' party? Teenage "music"?

Slip them on, and you'll feel like you're on a quiet beach (even if you're cowering in your study).

50

The number of full night's sleep a SuperDad will lose on average in his child's first year, according to *The Mirror*, 2024.

In addition to that loss, a typical parent spends

54 minutes a day

trying to get their baby to sleep* - more than a fortnight in their first year.

Just for the baby to wake up again four hours later.

A University of Oxford study showed that, in new mothers, areas of the brain located closer to the core – the regions responsible for nurture, caregiving and risk detection – showed the highest levels of activity.

In new dads, the outer surface of the brain was more active, where more conscious cognitive functions sit – such as goal setting, planning and problem-solving.

Source: New York Times, 2019

According to the *Independent*, SuperDads will pace the equivalent of two miles a day (and night) while rocking their baby to sleep.

That's more than 730 miles – the equivalent of 28 marathons! – in a year.

What do you call a girl standing between two posts?

Annette

SuperDad Motto #7

Take joy in the small things, like adding more cheese to your pizza (or any meal, really).

> "No drinking, no drugs, no kissing, no tattoos, no piercings, no ritual animal slaughters of any kind. Oh God, I'm giving them ideas."

Walter Stratford, *10 Things I Hate About You* (1999)
Directed by Gill Junger

Canadian dad Ted Hastings set a world-record for the most T-shirts worn at once – 260!

The idea for this bizarre challenge came about while Ted was flicking through the *Guinness World Records 2019*. When his young son dared him to set his own Guinness World Record title, Ted saw it as an opportunity to teach him an important lesson about hard work and commitment.

It just goes to prove, there aren't many things a father wouldn't do for his kids!

31 years old

The average age to become
a father in the U.S.

In 1972, it was

27 years old.

In the UK, the average age to
become a father is 33.8, rising
3.4 years since 1972.

I don't know who you are. I don't know what you want. If you are looking for ransom, I can tell you I don't have money, but what I do have are a very particular set of skills. Skills I have acquired over a very long career. Skills that make me a nightmare for people like you. If you let my daughter go now, that'll be the end of it. I will not look for you, I will not pursue you, but if you don't, I will look for you, I will find you and I will kill you.

Bryan Mills, *Taken* **(2008)**
Directed by Pierre Morel

What is black and white and black and white and black and white?

A penguin rolling down a hill

> 66

The only man a girl can depend on is her daddy.

> 99

Frenchy, *Grease* (1978)
Directed by Randal Kleiser

According to the Fatherhood Institute, British SuperDads now spend on average 55 minutes a day looking after their children – an increase of 18 per cent, or one-fifth, since 2015.

* For the first time in modern history, fathers now make up more than 10 per cent of the UK's stay-at-home parents.

1,042

The number of children the *Guinness Book of World Records* claims Moulan Ismail (Sultan of Morocco from 1672 to 1727) officially fathered in his lifetime – the highest number of children ever sired.

To help him achieve this feat, Moulin had four principle wives... and a harem of more than 500 friendly women.

Did you hear about the archaeologist who got fired?

His career is in ruins

> ❝
> # One father is more than a hundred schoolmasters.
> ❞

George Herbert
English poet and clergyman